DIVING BELL
Spiders

by Meg Gaertner

Content Consultant

Stefan K. Hetz
Department of Animal Physiology/Systems
Neurobiology and Neural Computation
Humboldt-Universität zu Berlin

CAPSTONE PRESS
a capstone imprint

Bright Idea Books are published by Capstone Press
1710 Roe Crest Drive, North Mankato, Minnesota 56003
www.mycapstone.com

Library of Congress Cataloging-in-Publication Data
Names: Gaertner, Meg, author.
Title: Diving bell spiders / by Meg Gaertner.
Description: North Mankato, Minnesota : Capstone Press, [2020] | Series:
   Unique animal adaptations | Audience: Grade 4 to 6. | Includes index.
Identifiers: LCCN 2018058424 (print) | LCCN 2018061653 (ebook) | ISBN
   9781543571660 (ebook) | ISBN 9781543571523 (hardcover) | ISBN
   9781543575064 (paperback)
Subjects: LCSH: Water spider--Juvenile literature. | Water
   spider--Adaptation--Juvenile literature.
Classification: LCC QL458.42.A75 (ebook) | LCC QL458.42.A75 G34 2020 (print)
   | DDC 595.76/3--dc23
LC record available at https://lccn.loc.gov/2018058424

All internet sites appearing in back matter were available and accurate when this book was sent
to press.

Editorial Credits
Editor: Marie Pearson
Designer: Becky Daum
Production Specialist: Colleen McLaren

Photo Credits
iStockphoto: DieterMeyrl, 6–7; Newscom: Stefan Hetz/CB2/ZOB/WENN.com, 26–27; Science
Source: Claude Nuridsany & Marie Perennou, 14–15, Dennis Kunkel Microscopy, 8, Francesco
Tomasinelli, 18–19, Steve Gschmeissner, 10–11; Shutterstock Images: D. Kucharski K. Kucharska,
17, Pavel Krasensky, cover; Stefan Hetz: 5, 13, 21, 22, 24–25, 28, 31

Design Elements: Shutterstock Images

Printed in the United States of America.
PA70

TABLE OF CONTENTS

CHAPTER 1

SPIDERS WITH
Diving Bells

Look at that spider in the water! It's a diving bell spider. It is also known as a water spider. It is the only spider that lives underwater.

An air bubble lets diving bell spiders live underwater.

5

Diving bell spiders live in Europe and Asia. They live in calm waters. These waters include ponds, marshes, and shallow lakes. Many water plants live in these areas. The spiders use the plants for their webs.

Some diving bell spiders live in ponds in Germany.

7

A magnified image of a diving bell spider shows its special hairs.

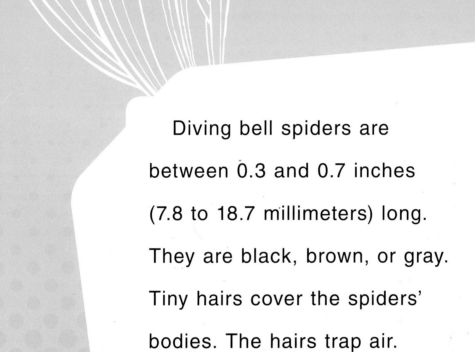

Diving bell spiders are
between 0.3 and 0.7 inches
(7.8 to 18.7 millimeters) long.
They are black, brown, or gray.
Tiny hairs cover the spiders'
bodies. The hairs trap air.

AIR BUBBLES

Diving bell spiders have **adapted** to their **environments**. Like most spiders, they get **oxygen** from air. But they bring air underwater. They do this by building their own diving bells.

DIVING BELLS

Humans used diving bells for thousands of years. These were large metal balls. They had an opening on the bottom. They trapped air inside them. Divers used the bells to breathe underwater.

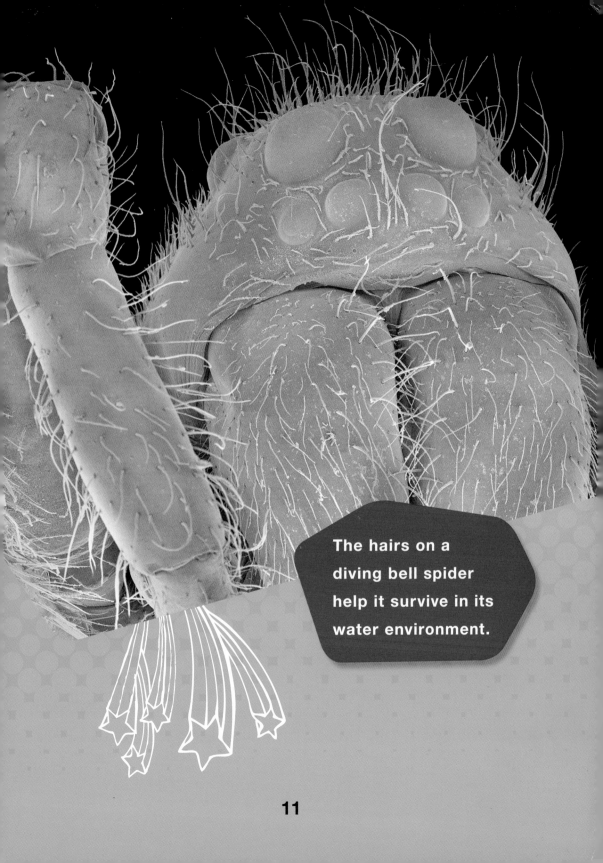

The hairs on a diving bell spider help it survive in its water environment.

CHAPTER 2

MAKING THE
Diving Bell

Before making a bell, the spider spins a curved web. It attaches the web to underwater plants. Then the spider swims to the water's surface. It uses hairs on its body and hind legs to trap air. The spider dives back down to the web. It brings a bubble of air with it. The spider releases the air bubble into the web. The web holds the bubble in place.

The diving bell spider crosses its legs behind its abdomen. This helps it trap a large bubble.

The air bubble
helps the spider
breathe underwater.

The spider makes many trips to the surface. It brings more air bubbles to its web. The bubbles become a single large one. It is big enough that the spider can fit inside. Now the spider has its own diving bell.

CHAPTER 3

BREATHING AND
Building

The water spider's bell holds air. It also works like a fish's **gill**. The bell has less oxygen than the water around it. Oxygen seeps into the bell. The bell stays full of oxygen.

16

The spider's bell releases carbon dioxide gas. The inside holds enough oxygen to breathe.

GILLS

A fish's gills are like lungs. Lungs pull oxygen from air. Gills pull oxygen from water. Then the oxygen enters the blood. The blood carries it around the body.

The spider carries air on its abdomen to its web.

The spider can stay inside its bell for a full day. Throughout a day, the bell shrinks. The spider senses this. It knows it must get more air. The spider swims to the water's surface. It brings new air bubbles back to the web. The bell gets bigger again.

CHAPTER 4

LIVING
Underwater

Diving bell spiders spend most of their lives in a bell. But sometimes they leave it. Their body hairs hold air close. The air lets the spiders breathe while swimming.

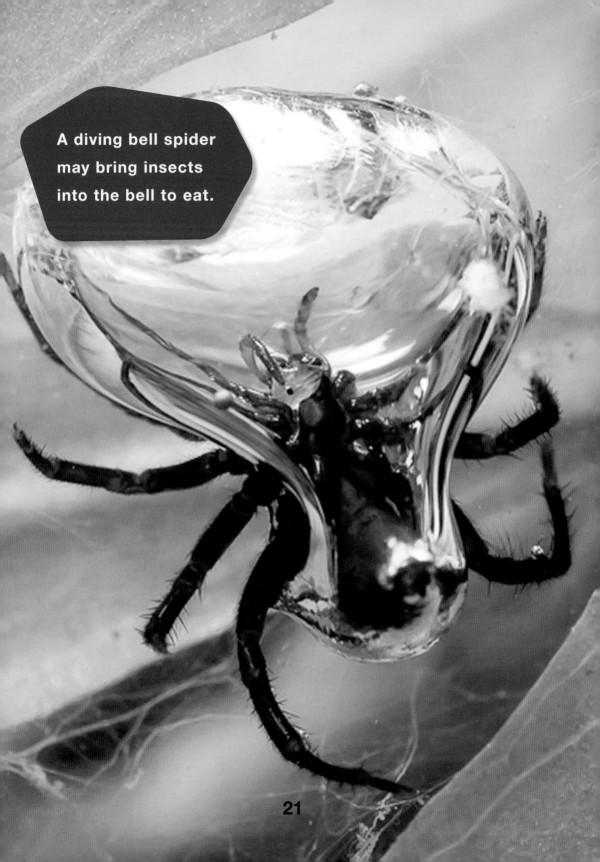

A diving bell spider may bring insects into the bell to eat.

Diving bell spiders
can hunt prey larger
than themselves.

Male spiders leave the bell to hunt for **prey**. They eat young insects and small fish. **Female** spiders wait for prey to come to them. A female spider surrounds her bell with silk. The silk moves when prey is nearby. The spider senses the movement. She jumps and grabs the prey. The spider pulls the prey into the bell to eat.

HIBERNATION

Diving bell spiders **hibernate** during cold winters. They dive deeper into the water. They build stronger bells. The new bells provide oxygen for four months.

BABIES

A male and female spider **mate**. A few hours later, the female makes an egg sac in the bell. Then the spider lays eggs. Each egg sac has up to 100 eggs. The spider stays with the eggs. It keeps them safe. Baby spiders hatch from the eggs after three or four weeks. The babies stay with their mother for two to four weeks. Then they leave. They build their own bells.

Baby spiders stay near
the bell after hatching.

Diving bell spiders are hard to study in the wild. This is because they live underwater. Scientists do not know how long wild spiders live. But **captive** ones live two years.

Scientists study spiders to learn more about them.

Scientists keep studying diving bell spiders. They learn more about the spiders' amazing adaptations.

GLOSSARY

adapt
to have differences that help a species fit into a new or different environment

captive
kept by humans

environment
the place where a person, plant, or animal lives

female
an animal of the sex that can lay eggs or have babies

gill
a body part of some animals that live in the water, such as fish, that pulls oxygen from water

hibernate
to spend the winter in an inactive state in order to survive the cold

male
an animal of the sex that cannot lay eggs or have babies

mate
to come together to have offspring

oxygen
a gas that all animals need to take in to survive

prey
an animal that is hunted by another animal

TRIVIA

1. In most types of spiders, females are bigger than males. Diving bell spiders are different. Male spiders are bigger. They are 0.31 to 0.74 inches (7.8 to 18.7 millimeters) long. Female spiders are less than 0.5 inches (13.1 mm) long.

2. Female diving bell spiders bring new air to their nests more often than males do.

3. Diving bell spiders are more active at night than during the day.

ACTIVITY

MAKE A DIVING BELL

Water spiders make diving bells by spinning webs and trapping air. But you can make your own diving bell right at home. Fill a large bowl with water. Then grab an empty glass. Turn the glass upside down. Gently lower it into the bowl of water. Be sure to keep the glass level. This will keep air trapped inside the glass. If you jerk the glass, the air will escape. Water will rush into the glass.

31

FURTHER RESOURCES

Curious about other cool spiders? Check out these resources:

DKfindout! Mexican Red-Kneed Tarantula
https://www.dkfindout.com/us/animals-and-nature/invertebrates/mexican-red-
 kneed-tarantula/

Furstinger, Nancy. *How Do Spiders Hear?* Crazy Animal Facts. North Mankato,
 Minn.: Capstone Publishing, 2019.

Want to know more about animal adaptations? Learn more here:

DKfindout! Animal Adaptations
https://www.dkfindout.com/us/video/animals-and-nature/animal-adaptation-
 video/

Royston, Angela. *Animals that Hide.* Adapted to Survive. Chicago: Capstone
 Raintree, 2014.

Wheeler-Toppen, Jodi. *Orchid Mantises and Other Extreme Insect Adaptations.*
 Extreme Adaptations. North Mankato, Minn.: Capstone Publishing, 2015.

INDEX